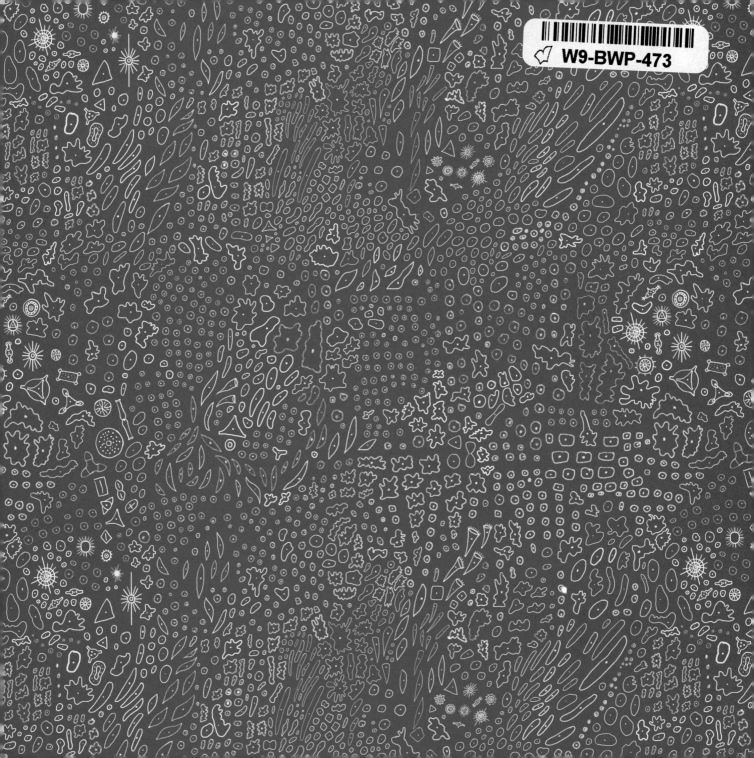

CELLS:
an OWNER'S
HANDBOOK

By Carolyn Fisher

Beach Lane Books • New York   London   Toronto   Sydney   New Delhi

HI! I'm Ellie.
No, not the dog.
Follow the arrow.

I'm a CELL!
A skin cell, actually.
A skin cell who lives on, er...

the derrière*
of a Boston terrier!
* Derrière is a fancy French word for butt.

Oh, you don't know what a CELL is???

Well, the dictionary* says that a cell is

"the smallest structural and functional unit of an organism, which is typically microscopic and consists of cytoplasm and a nucleus enclosed in a membrane."

Aren't you glad you asked???

* Oxford Dictionary of English (3rd edition) 2010

Wait a minute, can't you see me?

Hmm...Is that because we cells ARE SO SMALL that we're invisible to the naked eye?

LET'S ZOOM IN!

Here I am!

ELLIE the CELL
3,000 times magnification

Yeah, yeah, so I live on a dog's butt,

or as I like to call it, the *gluteus maximus*.

Let's carry on before we get, um, left behind!

CONGRATULATIONS!

You are the owner of 37 trillion

HIGH-PERFORMANCE

CELLS

(Pronounced "SELLS")

HUMAN: 37 trillion cells

ME: one skin cell
on the derrière
of a Boston terrier!

(give or take a few trillion).

Unicellular organisms* are made of just one cell.

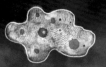

AMOEBA

PARAMECIUM

DIATOM

*An organism is an animal or plant.

Multicellular organisms

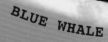

BLUE WHALE

...are made of MANY cells!

NON-LIVING THINGS
are NOT made of cells.

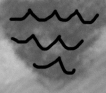

DIRT
Not made of cells

WATER
Not made of cells

ROCKS
Not made of cells

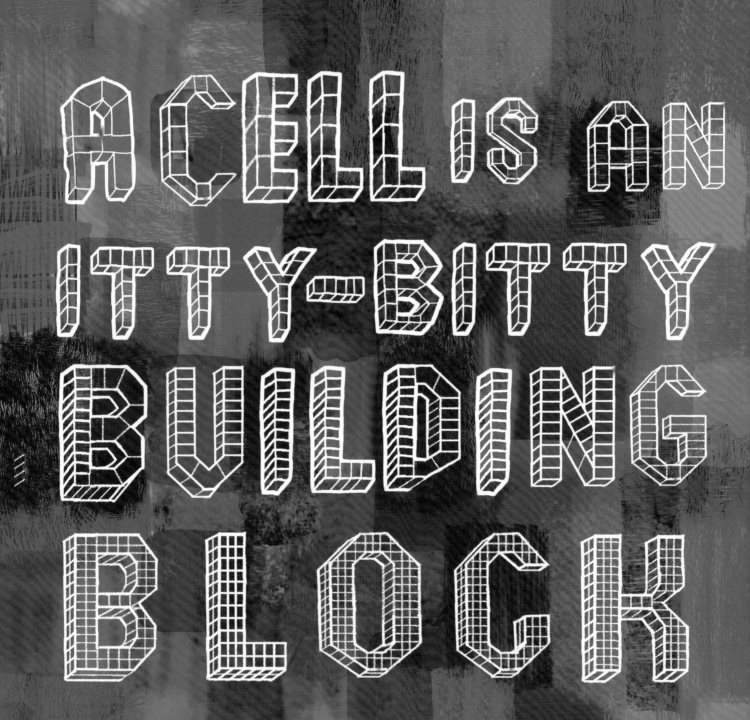

A CELL IS AN ITTY-BITTY BUILDING BLOCK

and...

everything else that's alive!

Most cells are so small
that you can't see them
unless you use a microscope*

*A microscope is a tool that helps magnify very tiny things

If your left little toe was this big,

a skin cell might be

THIS big.

↓

I, Ellie the cell, would be this big.

↓

(I'm tall for my age.)

If you looked at some of your cells through a microscope, you might see **this**

Skin cells, magnified 1,500 times

or this...

Nerve cells, magnified 500 times

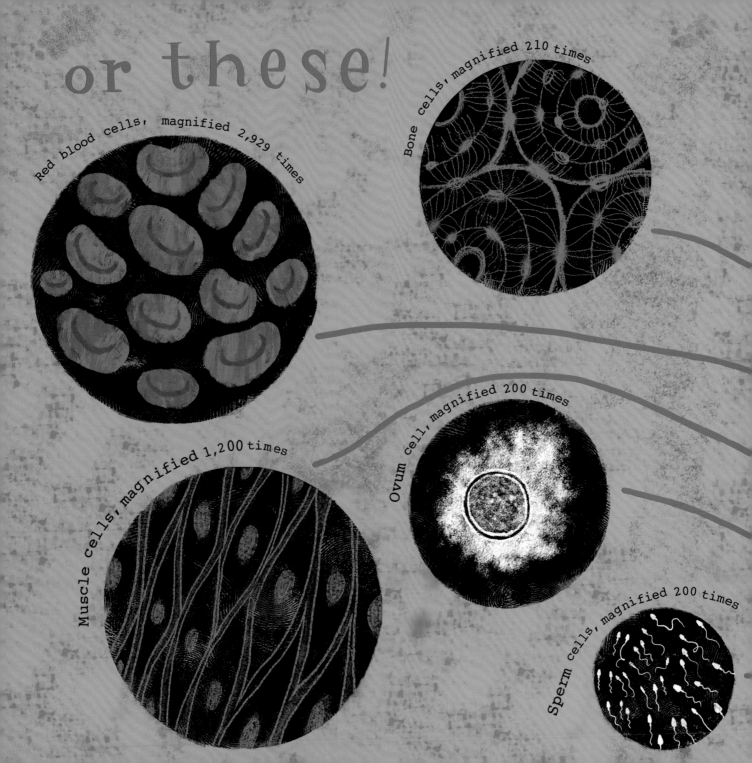

or these!

Red blood cells, magnified 2,929 times

Bone cells, magnified 210 times

Muscle cells, magnified 1,200 times

Ovum cell, magnified 200 times

Sperm cells, magnified 200 times

Different kinds of cells have different shapes and sizes to help them do different jobs like:

making bones,

making blood,

making muscles,

making babies!

Zoom in closer and one of your cells might look like THIS. →

CELL MEMBRANE
Encloses the cell's inside

Inside the cell, you'll find smaller parts called organelles (or-gan-ELZ).
Each organelle is a mini factory that does a special job.

LYSOSOMES:
(LIE-soh-soams)
Recycle old cell parts, bacteria, and viruses.

MITOCHONDRIA:
(mite-oh-KON-dree-yah)
Make energy for the cell.

NUCLEUS:
(NOO-klee-us)
CELL COMMAND CENTER
Holds instructions
(called DNA)
for making copies of cells
and building the body.

→DNA

RIBOSOMES:
(RYE-boh-soams)
Builders that make protein,
which is used to construct cells.

CYTOSOL:
(SY-toe-sol) The jelly-like stuff that holds
the organelles and nucleus.

ooh! If I'd known you were going to do a close-up, I would've combed my ribosomes!

CELLS MAKE NEW CELLS

(by copying themselves)...

TO GROW BODIES

and to REPAIR BODIES!

A time-lapse image of a cell

copying itself to make two new cells:

This is called MITOSIS (my-TOE-sis).

Some cells can divide two or three times per day.

Others split two or three times per year.

(Dead and worn-out cells are recycled and reused to make new cells.)

1 CELL WILL SPLIT INTO 2

2 CELLS will split into 4

4 CELLS WILL SPLIT INTO 8

8 CELLS will split into 16

16 CELLS WILL SPLIT INTO 32

32 CELLS will split into 64

64 CELLS WILL SPLIT INTO 128

128 CELLS will split into

256 CELLS WILL SPLIT

512 CELLS will

256
into 512
split into 1,024
and so on...

ALL THE PARTS OF A BODY HAVE THE NUMBER OF CELLS THEY NEED.*

brain

nerves

*If a cell keeps dividing without ever stopping, that can lead to a disease called cancer.

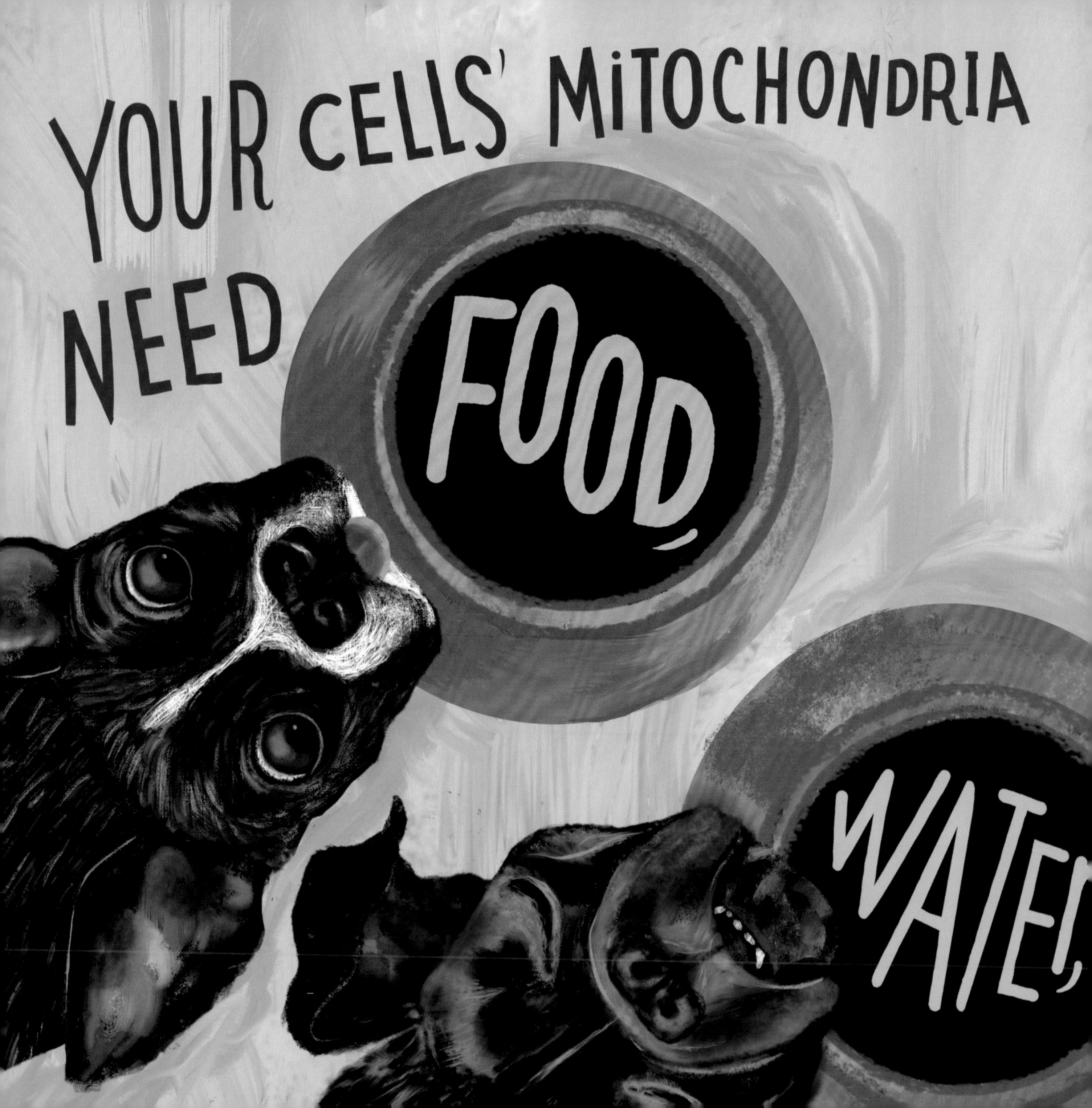
YOUR CELLS' MITOCHONDRIA NEED
FOOD,
WATER,

and **OXYGEN** to make energy for your body.

So eat, drink, and...

Lifetime
GUARANTEE

With proper recycling and replacement,
you should have enough cells
to last your whole life!

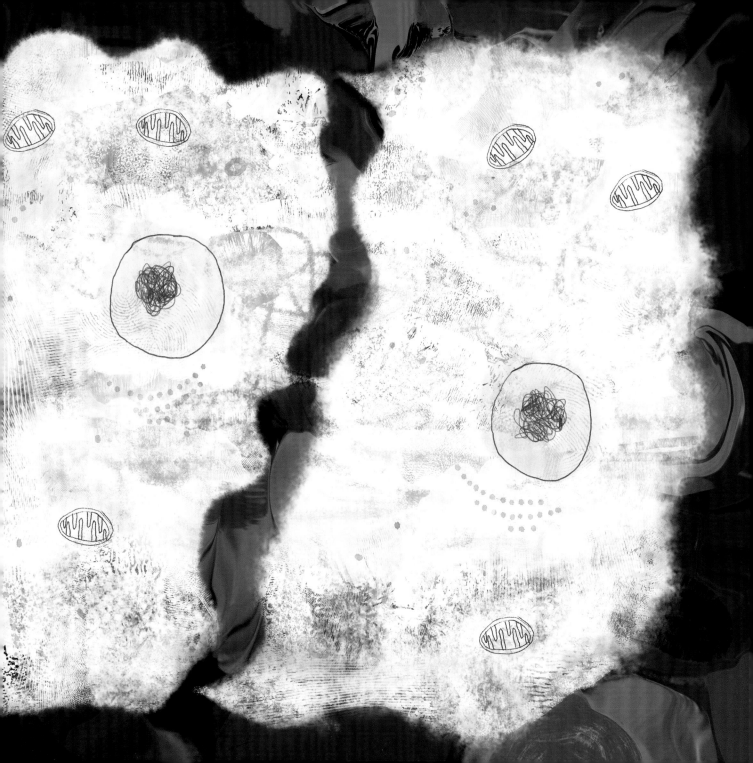

MORE on CELLS

ANIMAL CELLS VS. PLANT CELLS

- enclosed by a cell membrane
- make energy from food, water, and oxygen

- enclosed by a cell wall
- make energy from sunshine, water, and carbon dioxide

SOME UNICELLULAR ORGANISMS (That means one-celled, remember?)

AMOEBA
- enclosed by a cell membrane
- often lives in ponds, river bottoms, mud, and people
- makes energy from food, water, and oxygen

PARAMECIUM
- enclosed by a cell membrane
- often lives in fresh water
- makes energy from food, water, and oxygen

DIATOM
- enclosed by a shell
- lives in water
- makes energy from sunshine, water, and carbon dioxide

BACTERIA
- do not have a central nucleus
- live everywhere: in oceans, rivers, air, soil, plants, people, and more
- different bacteria make energy from different things, like cells, sunshine, people, plants, and more

A NOTE ON NUMBERS

Counting cells in a human body is hard, because cells are always moving or dividing or shedding. The estimate of 37.2 trillion cells in a human body comes from a 2013 study published in *Annals of Human Biology* by Eva Bianconi and 12 other scientists.

Eva Bianconi et al., "An estimation of the number of cells in the human body," *Annals of Human Biology* 40, no. 6 (2013): 463-471, https://doi.org/10.3109/03014460.2013.807878

37 TRILLION 3 JOKES

What is a cell's favorite subject in math?

D I V I S I O N!

Why did the microscope cross the road? To get to the other SLIDE!

KNOCK, KNOCK.
Who's there?
Mitosis.
Mitosis who?
Mitosis freezing out here. I forgot my shoes!

ADDITIONAL RESOURCES

Check out Bill Bryson's chapter on cells in *A Short History of Nearly Everything*.

Read Natalie Angier's musings on molecular biology in *The Canon: A Whirligig Tour of the Beautiful Basics of Science*.

Investigate microbes with Ed Yong's *I Contain Multitudes*.

Watch a TED-Ed animated video on the history of cell theory by Lauren Royal-Woods:
"The Wacky History of Cell Theory." ed.ted.com/lessons/the-wacky-history-of-cell-theory.

For Kieran

And for Christoph, Kirby, Quinn, Ellie, Keara, Riley, Avery, Hannah, and all the Calgary kids who read the story.

And especially for Steve.

A big thank-you to veterinary pathologist Dr. Cameron Knight of the University of Calgary, who was kind enough to look at the manuscript. (Any mistakes are mine, not his!)

BEACH LANE BOOKS • An imprint of Simon & Schuster Children's Publishing Division • 1230 Avenue of the Americas, New York, New York 10020 • Copyright © 2019 by Carolyn Fisher • All rights reserved, including the right of reproduction in whole or in part in any form. • BEACH LANE BOOKS is a trademark of Simon & Schuster, Inc. • For information about special discounts for bulk purchases, please contact Simon & Schuster Special Sales at 1-866-506-1949 or business@simonandschuster.com. • The Simon & Schuster Speakers Bureau can bring authors to your live event. For more information or to book an event, contact the Simon & Schuster Speakers Bureau at 1-866-248-3049 or visit our website at www.simonspeakers.com. • Book design by Carolyn Fisher • The text for this book was set in Futura. • The illustrations for this book were rendered digitally. • Manufactured in China • 0719 SCP • First Edition • 10 9 8 7 6 5 4 3 2 1 • Library of Congress Cataloging-in-Publication Data • Names: Fisher, Carolyn, author. • Title: Cells : an owner's handbook / Carolyn Fisher. • Description: First edition. | New York : Beach Lane Books, [2019] | Includes bibliographical references and index. | Audience: Age 3–8. | Audience: K to Grade 3. • Identifiers: LCCN 2019005536 | ISBN 9781534451858 (hardcover : alk. paper) | ISBN 9781534451827 (eBook) • Subjects: LCSH: Cells—Juvenile literature. • Classification: LCC QH582.5.F57 2019 | DDC 571.6—dc23 LC record available at https://lccn.loc.gov/2019005536

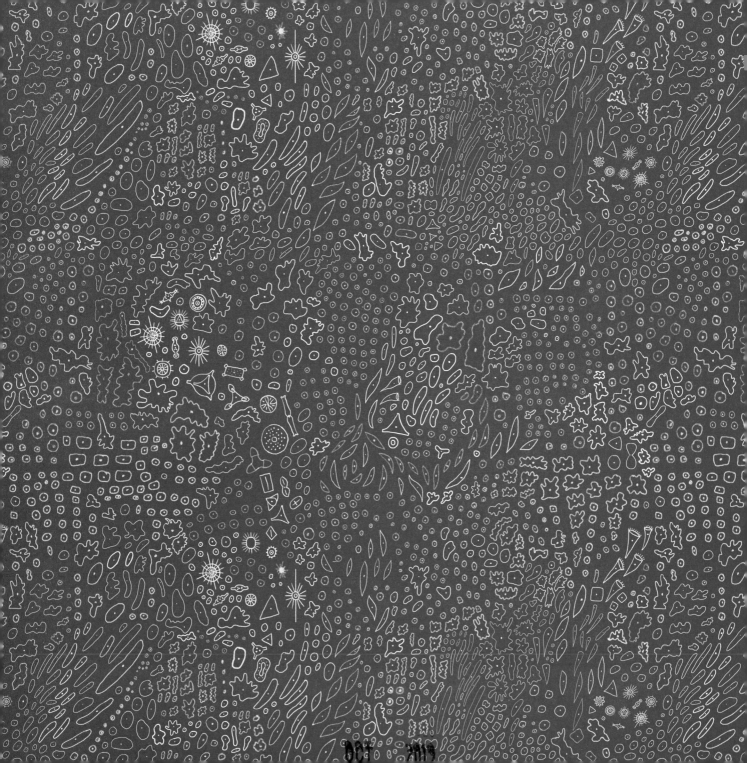